W9-AWS-566

BRAVE
ACTS

igloo

Samson

Judges 13-16

After many years of living in Canaan, the Hebrew people or, as they were later known, the Israelites, began worshipping false gods again. To punish them, God made them slaves of a people called the Philistines.

One day, an Israelite woman gave birth to a baby boy called Samson.
An angel had appeared to Samson's mother before his birth.
"Do not cut your child's hair," said the angel. "His long hair will give him strength, and show that he is destined to serve God."

When Samson grew up, he did indeed become very strong. Once, when a lion came roaring towards him, Samson killed it with his bare hands.

Over the years, Samson used his great strength against the Philistines and became their greatest enemy. He once killed a thousand Philistine soldiers, using only the jawbone of a donkey as a weapon.

When Samson fell in love with a girl called Delilah, the Philistines promised her money if she could discover the secret of his strength. Because he loved her, Samson told Delilah his secret.

"My strength lies in my long hair," he said. "If it were cut, I would be no stronger than any other man."

That night, Delilah allowed a Philistine in to where Samson was sleeping. The Philistine quickly cut off all of Samson's hair. When he woke, Samson realized that he had lost all of his strength. Then the Philistine soldiers burst in and put him into prison. But time passed and Samson's hair started to grow back again.

One day, the Philistines held a feast in one of their biggest Temples. They strung up Samson between two large pillars. Many people flocked to the Temple to laugh and jeer at him.
"Look at him!" they mocked. "Not so strong now!"
The crowd's teasing made Samson so angry he prayed to God to give him all his strength back. Then he pushed against the two pillars. The whole Temple collapsed under Samson's mighty strength. Samson was killed, but so, too, were the thousands of Philistines who had been inside the Temple with him.

It was Samson's last show of strength to the enemies of Israel.

David and Goliath

1 Samuel 16-17

Ruth's great grandson, David, worked on his father's farm. His job was to look after the sheep that grazed on the hills. He was a fearless boy who often had to defend his sheep against wild animals such as wolves and bears. He became an expert with a slingshot, which he fired stones with, to drive the wild animals away.

For years, King Saul of the Israelites had been fighting the Philistines. Down in the valley below David, a huge battle was about to take place. On one side of the valley lay the Israelite soldiers and, on the other, the mighty Philistine army.

One day, David's father asked him to take some food to his brothers who were soldiers in the Israelite army. As David got nearer, he could see the two great armies lined up opposite each other.

Suddenly, a giant of a man stepped out from the line of Philistine soldiers.

"My name is Goliath," he shouted to the Israelites. "I am the fiercest fighter in the world! No one can beat me! I challenge one of you to fight me! If you win, you win the battle for your whole army!"

The Israelite soldiers shrank back in fear. None of them dared to fight Goliath alone. Then David stepped forward.

"I'll fight you," he said. "I'm not afraid of you."

Goliath threw his head back and roared with laughter.

"Don't be silly, little boy. I will kill you in an instant."

"No, you won't," replied David. "I have God on my side."

King Saul tried to persuade David not to fight, but David's reply was simple and brave:

"Do not worry, my King. God will help me."

Saul gave David his armour, but it was far too heavy for him to wear.

"I just need my slingshot and my faith in God," said David. Then the giant and the boy walked out to fight each other. David bent down and picked up five smooth stones from the river bed. All of a sudden, Goliath charged at him with a huge roar. David carefully loaded his slingshot with one of the stones, took aim and fired it at the giant. The stone hit Goliath right between the eyes, and buried deep in his forehead. He was stopped in an instant and fell dead at David's feet.

The Philistines could not believe that their hero, Goliath, was dead. The Israelites cheered their new hero, David, and chased the Philistine soldiers all the way back to their city gates. David was his country's saviour. He became famous throughout the land and eventually, when he grew up, became King of Israel.

King Solomon

1 King 1-3

When King David became very old and weak, he took to ruling Israel from his bed. He knew that death was near, and wanted to be sure that the throne would pass into a safe pair of hands.

Years before, he had promised God that his son, Solomon, would be the new King when he died. But another of David's sons, Adonijah, grew ambitious and wanted the throne for himself.

When eventually Solomon did become King, Adonijah was afraid that Solomon might punish him for wanting the crown for himself. But Solomon told Adonijah that he would not harm him as long as he remained a good man.

Most of all, Solomon wanted to be wise. When God appeared to him in a dream, Solomon asked Him for the gift of wisdom. God promised He would make Solomon wise and, because Solomon asked for nothing but wisdom, God also promised him great wealth and a long life.

One day, two women came to see King Solomon. They had a baby with them, and each woman said that the baby belonged to her. They wanted Solomon to decide who was the real mother.

"Bring me a sword," said Solomon. "I will cut the baby in half. In this way, you can share this child," he told the women.

One of the women agreed to this at once, but the other cried out, "No! I would rather see my baby brought up by another woman than see my child killed."

Solomon now knew for sure that this woman was the baby's true mother. Only the real mother would allow the child to be brought up by someone else rather than see it die.

"Take your baby," he said, handing the infant to the woman, "and go in peace."

God had been true to His word. He had made Solomon a great leader, and all the people of Israel marvelled at his wisdom.

Daniel and the Lions

Daniel 1, 6

Many people still disobeyed God's commands, so God allowed the King of Babylon to invade Judah. A lot of people were taken back to Babylon as prisoners. Among them was a small boy called Daniel. He came from a noble family. The King of Babylon wanted children from noble families to be given a good education, so that they would be useful to Babylon in the future.

So Daniel was educated, and treated well while he was growing up, but he never forgot that he was from Judah, and prayed to God three times a day.

When the Persians invaded Babylon, their King, Darius, began to rule the country. By this time, Daniel had grown up and was famous for being a wise and popular man. King Darius liked Daniel so much he made him one of the three rulers of the whole country. But the other two rulers were jealous of Daniel and wanted to be rid of him.

Knowing that Daniel still prayed three times a day to God, the other two rulers made a new law. This law said that for the next thirty days, people should only pray to King Darius. If anyone broke this law they would be fed to the lions. So the jealous rulers went to Darius and told him that Daniel was still praying to God, and therefore, Daniel must die.

As much as Darius liked Daniel, he knew he could not save him. The very next day Daniel was thrown into the lions' pit and a large rock was pushed over the opening. That night, Darius was so worried for Daniel that he could not sleep.

Early the next morning, Darius rushed to the lions' pit and had the rock pushed back.

"Are you still alive, my friend?" he shouted into the pit, fearing the worst.

"I am!" cried Daniel. "My God knew I had done you no wrong and has kept me alive!"